SPORTS ALL-STARS

VON MILLER

Jon M. Fishman

Lerner Publications ◆ Minneapolis

Lerner Publications Company
A division of Lerner Publishing Group, Inc.
241 First Avenue North
Minneapolis, MN 55401 USA

For reading levels and more information, look up this title at www.lernerbooks.com.

Main body text set in Albany Std 15/22. Typeface provided by Agfa.

Library of Congress Cataloging-in-Publication Data

Names: Fishman, Jon M., author.
Title: Von Miller / Jon M. Fishman.
Description: Minneapolis : Lerner Publications, [2018] | Series: Sports All-Stars | Includes bibliographical references and index. | Audience: Ages: 7–11. | Audience: Grades: 4 to 6.
Identifiers: LCCN 2016058434 (print) | LCCN 2017005776 (ebook) | ISBN 9781512434552 (lb : alk. paper) | ISBN 9781512456202 (pb : alk. paper) | ISBN 9781512450910 (eb pdf)
Subjects: LCSH: Miller, Von, 1989—Juvenile literature. | Football players—Biography—Juvenile literature. | Denver Broncos (Football team)—History—Juvenile literature.
Classification: LCC GV939.M52 F57 2018 (print) | LCC GV939.M52 (ebook) | DDC 796.332092 [B] —dc23

LC record available at https://lccn.loc.gov/2016058434

Manufactured in the United States of America
1-42105-25398-3/29/2017

CONTENTS

"A GREAT, GREAT PLAYER"

Von Miller (center) closes in on Colts quarterback Andrew Luck (left).

Von Miller of the Denver Broncos leaned forward. The **linebacker** watched the football. He and his teammates were lined up against the Indianapolis Colts on September 18, 2016. *Hut-hut!* Broncos and Colts smashed into one another as the play began.

Colts quarterback Andrew Luck looked for an open teammate to throw the ball to. He tried to get rid of the ball quickly. But he wasn't fast enough. Miller cut through the **offensive line**. He stayed low to the ground and streaked toward Luck. Miller wrapped his arms around the quarterback and dragged him to the ground. **Sack!**

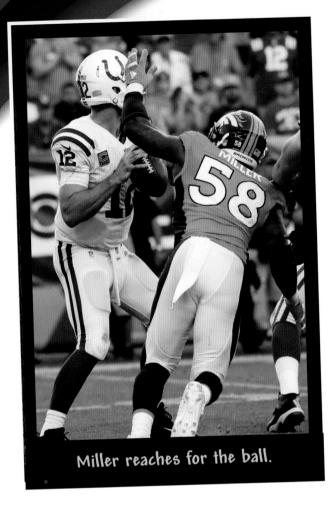
Miller reaches for the ball.

Miller was the best player on the best defense in the National Football League (NFL). The Broncos had won Super Bowl 50 earlier that year. Miller was voted the game's Most Valuable Player (MVP). The Denver offense was good. But most fans agreed that the hard-hitting defense made the team great.

The Colts weren't pushovers. They scored a touchdown with about four minutes left in the game to make the score Denver 23, Indianapolis 20. After the Broncos kicked a **field goal**, the score stood at 26–20. But Indianapolis got the ball back with just under two minutes left to play. A touchdown could win the game for the Colts. This time, the Broncos had to stop them.

Denver fans were uneasy as the Colts lined up for their first play. But Miller quickly gave them something to cheer about. He shot forward like a cannonball. He stepped to his right, then cut left. The Colts player who tried to block him had no chance.

Miller had an open path to Andrew Luck. But instead of knocking him to the ground, Miller swatted the ball out of Luck's hands. It bounced to a Denver teammate who sprinted 15 yards for a touchdown! The play sealed the win for Denver.

Colts coach Chuck Pagano talked about the play after the game. "It was Von Miller being Von Miller," Pagano said. "He's a great, great player and he made a great, great play."

Miller (left) celebrates with Broncos teammate Derek Wolfe (right) after sacking Andrew Luck.

Football fans take in a high school game in Texas. High school football is a very big deal there!

Vonnie B'Vsean Miller Jr. was born in DeSoto, Texas, on March 26, 1989. His friends and family called him Von. DeSoto is in the heart of football country. Even local youth games are a big deal. People often show up hours before such games to **tailgate** and have fun.

Von wanted to play football. But he was skinny and wore glasses. His dad said no. He wanted Von to grow stronger before taking up such a tough sport. So instead, Von asked his mom.

"Mom," Von said. "Mom. Mom, come on. I'll make my bed every day. I'll mow the lawn. Mom, just let me play football. I'm ready!"

Miller walks off the field with his mom, Gloria, after Super Bowl 50.

Von's mom finally agreed to let him play. They didn't tell his dad at first. Von loved to smash into people on the football field, but his glasses were a problem. They kept falling off his face during plays. Von kept his glasses in place by wrapping goggles around the outside of his helmet.

These days, Miller uses his glasses as a fashion statement.

At DeSoto High School, Von grew into a fearsome player. **Scouts** ranked him as one of the top high school talents in the United States. College was the next step. He got offers from big-time football schools such as the University of Florida and the University of Oklahoma. Von stayed close to home and enrolled at Texas A&M University.

Miller won the Butkus Award in 2010 as the best linebacker in college football. In 2011, he entered the NFL **Draft**. The Denver Broncos chose him with the second overall pick. The skinny kid with glasses had made it all the way to football's top level.

Miller went to DeSoto High School with three friends: Tony Jerod-Eddie, Damontre Moore, and Cyrus Gray. All four played together at Texas A&M. Then the four friends all made it to the NFL.

Miller runs even on his way to practice!

During the season, Miller gets plenty of exercise. When he isn't chasing quarterbacks around the field, he's practicing, lifting light weights, and stretching with the team. But in the NFL's off-season, he's on his own.

Miller tackles a blocking pad during practice.

That doesn't mean Miller slows down much. Not even winning the Super Bowl MVP award stopped him. "I really didn't just take days off," Miller said. "Right after the Super Bowl, I started working out." He exercises every day except Saturday and Sunday, even when there are no games to prepare for. He does sprints and other exercises to improve his speed and balance. As the season nears, Miller hits the gym to lift heavy weights and build up his muscles.

When you exercise as much as Miller does, you need to take in a lot of **protein**. Protein helps rebuild muscles. To get all he needs, Miller drinks protein shakes after workouts. Some of the shakes taste terrible. But Miller doesn't care. "I just need that fuel," he said.

Miller didn't think much about his diet in college. He ate a lot of hamburgers and Chick-fil-A sandwiches. In the NFL, coaches and trainers put him on a more healthful track. He gave up most of the junk food and sugary snacks he ate in college. Instead of soda, Miller drinks juices and at least a gallon of water each day.

Miller makes sure to drink plenty of water during workouts and team practices.

One of Miller's favorite foods is eggs. He likes to have four eggs with turkey bacon, fruit, and a potato for breakfast. Lunch is something different every day, but it always includes a lot of protein. A large chicken breast with brown rice is often on the menu. Dinner is more protein such as fish along with vegetables. He eats a lot of broccoli, both cooked and raw.

Miller sticks to his healthful diet *almost* all the time. But sometimes he cuts loose and has a cheat day, as he calls it. On those days, he eats whatever sounds good. He may have a soda and ice cream. Pizza, mashed potatoes, and macaroni and cheese are also high on Miller's cheat-day list.

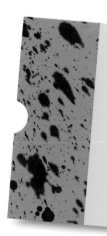

Miller's favorite snack is beef jerky. He carries some with him throughout the day. It's delicious, and of course, it's packed with protein.

Miller dressed the part for the 2016 Academy of Country Music Awards.

Chickens have a good home on Miller Farms.

Von Miller loves chickens. And not just to eat. He raises them with his family in DeSoto. At Miller Farms, the chickens run free and lay eggs for Miller's big breakfasts. He even has plans to expand his farm into a business.

When he's not collecting eggs or sacking quarterbacks, Miller lives like a superstar. Maybe you saw him on TV at the *Academy of Country Music Awards*. He presented an award dressed liked a cowboy.

On *Dancing with the Stars*, he performed dressed as Michael Jackson and Elvis Presley. The costumes didn't save him from being voted off the show, though. In 2016, Miller got his first acting job as a guest on *Saturday Night Live*.

Miller struts his stuff on the dance floor on *Dancing with the Stars*.

Miller showed off more moves in a funny commercial for the *Madden NFL 17* video game. He danced and sang and wore a bunch of wild outfits. He likes to dress up even when he isn't onstage. He's known for wearing flashy hats and unusual T-shirts. In 2016, *Sports Illustrated* magazine named him the NFL's "Most Fashionable Star."

Miller is known for his colorful outfits and fun style.

Miller and his teammates listen to then president Obama speak during their 2016 visit to the White House.

Each year the team that won the Super Bowl goes to the White House to meet the president of the United States. Miller and his Denver teammates traveled there a few months after winning the 2016 Super Bowl. They spoke with then president Barack Obama. The president "talked about how cool he thought my

Giving Back

In July 2016, five police officers in Dallas, Texas, lost their lives to violence. Miller wanted to do something to help. The next day, he gave a brand-new, specially made car to the DeSoto Police Department. He went to the police station to meet the officers and sign autographs. He also gave $25,000 to the town's fire department

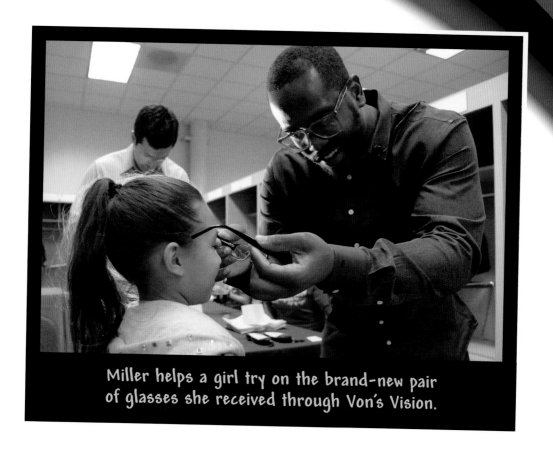

Miller helps a girl try on the brand-new pair of glasses she received through Von's Vision.

shoes are and my dance moves," Miller said.

Miller's life off the field isn't all dancing and chicken farming. He knows firsthand how important it is for kids with vision problems to have good glasses. So he started Von's Vision. The group helps kids in Denver get the eyewear they need. They also hold events that provide free eye exams. In November 2016, Miller hosted a dinner called Von Miller's Celebrity Steak-Out with some of his teammates. The event raised almost $500,000 for Von's Vision!

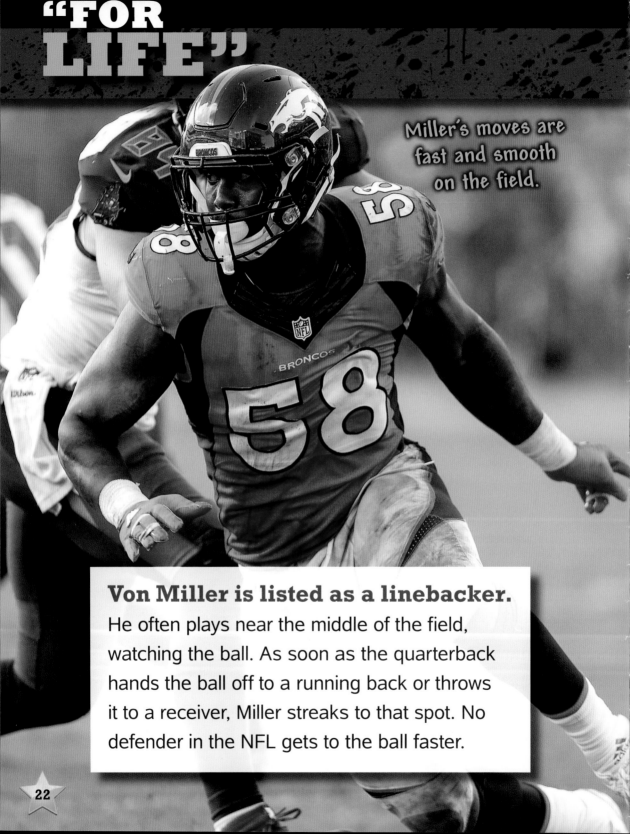

"FOR LIFE"

Miller's moves are fast and smooth on the field.

Von Miller is listed as a linebacker. He often plays near the middle of the field, watching the ball. As soon as the quarterback hands the ball off to a running back or throws it to a receiver, Miller streaks to that spot. No defender in the NFL gets to the ball faster.

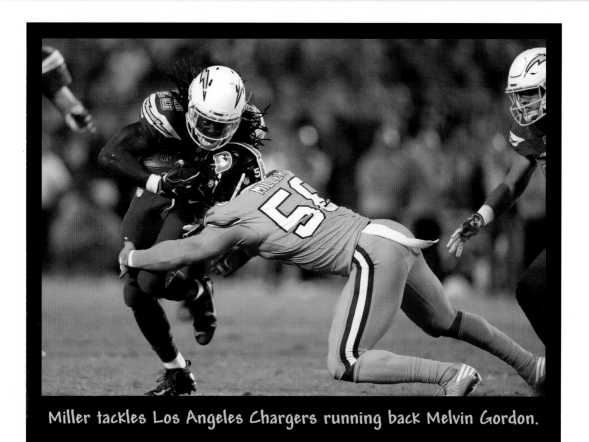

Miller tackles Los Angeles Chargers running back Melvin Gordon.

Sometimes Miller plays on the **defensive line**. He's strong enough to take on gigantic offensive linemen. He may knock them to the ground. Other times, he pushes them back into their own quarterbacks. When that doesn't work, Miller simply runs by them. His speed makes him special.

When he gets within reach of a quarterback, Miller brings him down without mercy. Then it's time to dance. Miller's sack-dance celebrations are even more famous than his *Dancing with the Stars* moves.

Miller busts a move after sacking a quarterback.

Miller raises the Vince Lombardi Trophy after helping the Broncos win Super Bowl 50.

Miller was just 26 years old when the Broncos won Super Bowl 50. Yet he had already accomplished so much. The Defensive Rookie of the Year award. Four **Pro Bowls**. The Super Bowl MVP award. On April 16, 2016, his hometown of DeSoto gave him another honor. The mayor named it Von Miller Day.

It was time for Miller to get paid like one of the world's best football players. His **contract** was due to end after the 2016 season. Miller and his **agents** tried to strike a new deal with Denver. But the two sides couldn't agree. Miller missed some off-season practices while the sides argued. Then, in July 2016, he agreed to a deal. The new contract would keep him in Denver through the 2021 season.

Miller gets fired up with his team before a game.

Miller celebrates yet another sack!

And it would pay him a whopping $114.5 million. Only Andrew Luck's contract was worth more money at the time.

Miller was happy to focus on football again. "FOR LIFE," he wrote on Twitter after signing his new contract. The deal would keep him in Denver for most of his career—he would be a Bronco for life. He added a picture to the tweet that showed him wearing his uniform with his fist in the air. It's a sight Broncos fans have gotten used to and one they'll get to see a lot more in the future.

Most Career Sacks in Broncos History

Player	Sacks
Simon Fletcher	97.5
Karl Mecklenburg	79
Von Miller	73.5
Trevor Pryce	64
Elvis Dumervil	63.5
Rulon Jones	52.5
Maa Tanuvasa	33
Alfred Williams	28.5
Barney Chavous	23
Bill Romanowski	23

Source Notes

7 "Miller's Sack-Strip Leads Broncos Past Colts," *ESPN*, September 18, 2016, http://www.espn.com/nfl/recap?gameId=400874526.

9 Von Miller, "Nerd," *Players' Tribune*, February 18, 2016, http://www.theplayerstribune.com/von-miller-broncos-super-bowl-mvp-nerd.

13 Andrew Mason, "Von Miller Hopes His Altered Diet Yields Better Results," Denver Broncos, April 15, 2015, http://www.denverbroncos.com/news-and-blogs/article-1/Von-Miller-hopes-his-altered-diet-yields-better-results/d76ae2b5-cf3f-478b-aaa7-fecce80f14a0.

14 Mick Rouse, "The Real-Life Diet of Von Miller, Who Always Eats Clean," *GQ*, November 29, 2016, http://www.gq.com/story/real-life-diet-von-miller.

20–21 Sam Alipour, "Hang Time: A Q&A with Von Miller, Super Bowl-Winning Chicken Farmer," *ESPN*, July 14, 2016, http://www.espn.com/nfl/story/_/id/17078455/denver-bronco-von-miller-life-chicken-farmer.

Glossary

agents: people who represent athletes in business deals

contract: an agreement between a player and a team that states how much a player will be paid and how long the player will be with the team

defensive line: the players at the front of the defense who face off against the offensive line

draft: a yearly event in which teams take turns choosing new players

field goal: a kick that goes between the goalposts at either end of the field. A field goal is worth three points.

linebacker: a defender who usually covers the middle of the field

offensive line: the five players at the front of the offense whose main job is to block defenders

Pro Bowls: NFL all-star games

protein: a substance in foods such as meat and beans that the body needs

sack: to tackle the quarterback for a loss of yards

scouts: people who judge the skills of athletes

tailgate: a social gathering where people meet in parking lots before sporting events to eat and play games

Fishman, Jon M. *Andrew Luck*. Minneapolis: Lerner Publications, 2014.

Gitlin, Marty. *Von Miller: Football Star*. Mankato, MN: North Star Editions, 2017.

NFL Rush
http://www.nflrush.com

Scheff, Matt. *Superstars of the Denver Broncos*. Mankato, MN: Amicus, 2014.

Sports Illustrated Kids
http://www.sikids.com

Von's Vision
http://www.vonmiller.org

Index

Photo Acknowledgments

The images in this book are used with the permission of: © iStockphoto.com/63151 (gold and silver stars); Cliff Welch/Icon Sportswire 357/Newscom, p. 2; © Dustin Bradford/Getty Images, pp. 4, 26; © John Leyba/The Denver Post/Getty Images, pp. 6, 7, 13, 14, 21, 24; Eric S. Swist/Icon SMI/Newscom, p. 8; AP Photo/Jae C. Hong, p. 9; © Frazer Harrison/Getty Images, p. 10; © Brent Lewis/The Denver Post/ Getty Images, p. 12; © Denise Truscello/Getty Images, p. 16; © iStockphoto.com/ monticelllo, p. 17; © Adam Taylor/ABC/Getty Images, p. 18; © Jeff Vespa/WireImage/ Getty Images, p. 19; © Cheriss May/NurPhoto/Getty Images, p. 20; © Don Juan Moore/Getty Images, p. 22; © Sean M. Haffey/Getty Images, p. 23; © Ezra Shaw/ Getty Images, p. 25; © Joe Amon/The Denver Post/Getty Images, p. 27.

Front cover: Cliff Welch/Icon Sportswire 357/Newscom, © iStockphoto.com/ neyro2008 (motion lines).